"From the Basement to the Stage"

I Am the Arts

Darnell Richardson Jr.

I AM THE ARTS

WRITTEN BY: Darnell Richardson Jr.

© 2020

PUBLISHED BY: Pen Legacy, LLC
TYPESETTING & LAYOUT BY: The Liar's Craft
COVER BY: Christian Cuan
STORY EDITING BY: Carla M. Dean, U Can Mark My Word

Library of Congress Cataloging – in- Publication Data has been applied for.

ISBN: 978-1-7348278-4-2

PRINTED IN THE UNITED STATES OF AMERICA.

This Book is Dedicated to my grandmother Mildred Taylor.

Table of Contents

"I am going to create a job for myself in your company."

~ Darnell Richardson Jr.

Acknowledgements

First, I want to give honor and praise to my God for keeping me grounded on Your mission for my life. I owe my journey to You, and I continue to ask You to protect, watch, and provide me with Your mercy.

To my grandmother, Mildred Taylor, you have been amazing. Even when you didn't understand at times, you trusted the process and waited for the results.

To my mother, Andrea Taylor, and father, Darnell Richardson Sr., thank you for giving birth to me and bringing me into this world.

To Aunt Kathy Richardson-Graham, Aunt Robin Brown, Spiritual Sister Patricia Curry, Spiritual Grandma Linda Rich, Dr. Stacy Gill Philips, and God Mom Elaine Johnson, I appreciate you for being in my life and adding great value in many different ways.

To my Imhotep parents, Baba Tyrone Davis and Mama Christine Wiggins, I could not have made this decision and trusted the process without your teachings. You set the standards and passed the torch. Thank you.

To my Sisters, Niece & Nephews & Everyone who supported my journey. Thank you!

Rest in Peace, Grandma Lilian Richardson & Grandma Yolanda, I pray you are proud of my accomplishments. I've listened, learned, and am living my life, my way.

Accomplishments

2010

- May 10th, 2010 - Official Formation of D. Richardson Productions LLC
- Started D. Richardson Productions Dance Academy, formally Danse4Ever
- Traveled to Ghana, West Africa

2011

- Produced for stage production *Girl He Loves Me* at the Walking Fish Theatre in Philadelphia, PA
- Learned the party entertainment business professionally
- Started teaching performing arts course at West Philadelphia Achievement Charter

2012

- Produced 2nd stage play *Faith of a Mustard Seed* in Philadelphia, PA
- Started my TV show, *I Am a Philly Artist TV*
- D. Richardson Productions became a LLC.

2013

- Attended Full Sail University - Entertainment Business Major

2014

- Hosted a Christian radio show with Rev. Linda Gusoff, PWLC

- Moved to Smyrna, Delaware

2015

- Restage *Faith of a Mustard Seed* in a 260-seat state-of-art theatre
- Joined Groove Phi Groove Social Fellowship Incorporated
- Produced *The Reassurance* stage play

2016

- Created a circus production during Christmastime
- Added multiple locations to the dance academy

2017

- Revamped the D. Richardson Productions brand with more services
- Worked as Executive Staff for the 6ABC Thanksgiving Day Parade

2018

- Performed Magic Show Center Court at the Wells Fargo Center during the Harlem Globetrotters game

2019

- Went back to school at Full Sail University
- Started writing the book *From the Basement to the Stage*

2020

- Opened event space/dance academy in Brewerytown community

- Relocated from Philadelphia to South Florida as second home

- Nominated for Industry Professional Award

When God Says It's Time, It's Time!

I know you are saying to yourself, "What in the world is Darnell up to now?" To be honest, God is indeed the master and creator of my destiny, and nothing I do was ever planned! He knew what I needed to propel my dreams and aligned me in front of those who were assigned to make it happen. Some people have prayed a lifetime to receive all that I have accomplished before the age of thirty. Now, I have a book with my name on it. Can you feel my excitement through these words? It has been almost a four-year journey, but I am grateful I stayed on course. Thank God for a cousin who kept a spot open for me on her calendar, no matter how many times I told her that I was going to publish and didn't follow through. But, hey, when God says it's time, it's time.

Allow me to introduce myself. My name is Darnell Richardson, Jr., son of Andrea Taylor and Darnell Richardson, Sr. Like many of you, my parents had their blueprint for my life. They threw every weapon to deter me, but God made sure none of them prospered. As a kid, I was very inquisitive and had a creative imagination. I was the kid who would raise their hand when a new, cool opportunity presented itself. You know, the one who volunteered for everything? Yeah, that was me. I wasn't interested in pursuing these things later as a career. I was merely satisfying my curiosity. Once my satisfaction was peaked, I took the information provided and ran with it. Using my imagination, I would then create my rendition of what I witnessed, adding my spin and flavor to it.

Growing up in North Philadelphia during a time when there was no internet, we did not have a computer or the luxury of cable. Antenna programming and toys were my favorite pastimes. I spent a lot of time by myself playing and pretending. What do you do when playing make-believe leads you to consider making it your reality but as an entrepreneur? How do you persuade your mother that the arts are your dream job? If you had a mother like mine, who believed anything in entertainment was not promising and immediately dismissed it, you were ordered to get a real job. How do you live with that? Well, for me, it was a challenge that caused me to find refuge in others and the activities at school. I turned from her disapproval to acceptance by others and used their knowledge, platform, and assistance to steer me in the right direction. That direction has me celebrating ten years as an entrepreneur this year. Trust me when I say it was a long, hard road to get here. But, by the grace of God, I made it, and the next ten is looking mighty global.

Now I know you may be thinking, *How in the world did he do that?* Well, I'm glad you asked. It is my intention not only to share my testimony but give you the ugly truth of what many of us dreamers have to go through. This book is written by a little boy who had a big imagination and used grit, determination, and sacrifice to hear his own. Yes, at times, I had to be destructive to get the job done. When you know what you want, desperate times call for desperate measures. There were many times when I could have gotten chastised for what many considered unruly behavior, but I had supportive people in my life, such as my grandmother, who celebrated it all with a smile.

As you take the journey with me from the "**Basement to Entrepreneurship**", use these words as a means of great lessons and inspiration. Channel inward to find your childhood desires. What were your gifts and talents? What did you enjoy doing that could now serve as a stream of income? When you find that place, then give birth to the reason why you quit. Who told you that you would never make it? Is the lack of money costing you your dreams? What if I told you that by the end of this book, you would be motivated to jumpstart your dreams by at least being able to speak your goal. Many of you are stuck in the routine called life because you haven't allowed yourself the opportunity to speak and manifest your vision. If you could achieve anything today and it not cost you anything, what would it be? Now take that same thought and write it down. Then, I challenge you every day to do something that will lead to you witnessing the birth of what you initially thought was impossible. It is my hope that my journey disrupts your buried dreams and offers you the oxygen needed to breathe life into your dead vision.

As you read each chapter, please remember that I was only a child that turned lack into a passion and now a career. I walked blindly, faithfully toward what could be by utilizing my gift of exploration and then my ability to create. Nothing was handed to me. I had to fight, beg, and hustle my way to where I am today. I failed, lost, and was denied, but what I know to be true is that "I can do all things through Christ who strengthens me." (Philippians 4:13) From sleeping on couches to opening up for Beyoncé, I made it. In this book, I will show you ways that you can, too, by sharing my lessons and offering you five keys to staying in your lane to success. Being an entrepreneur already has its challenges, and if I can alleviate some of the pain and burden for you, then this whole writing process has been worth it. Now, you may have a few questions or want to chat with me after reading, and that can definitely be arranged. If this book or any moment resonates with you, let's have a conversation and possibly see how we can use that resonation to spark something greater.

In addition, I detail the many lessons I learned and how I had to rebuild my life after entrepreneurship almost took me out. Sadly, social media only offers you the glamorous side of this world. I will share with you the broke and brokenness I suffered while escaping a lawsuit at the age of eighteen, surviving homelessness, and learning how to build a business with no formal education. When I tell you, life for me has been no crystal stair. Even though I penned this book from a place of love, nothing you have ever read is rawer and more uncut than this. It's no holds barred, and for the first time in life, I am excited to finally be releasing the joys and pain of what many think was a walk in the park.

I am truly grateful for this opportunity to share my truth with you all. I know many of you who are reading this will be shocked, while others will be proud that I persevered. No matter how you respond, I want to leave you with the two mantras that carried me throughout everything: "Never let anyone talk you out of your dreams" and "Life is a big oyster; there is nothing wrong with exploring the waters to see where you fit." These affirmations were the fuel that kept me going despite what was going on in and around me. Many tried to steer me away from my goal, but there were tons of relatives, strangers, and colleagues who spoke praise against the negativity. I have had people step up, like Ms. Patricia Curry, who asked, "What do you need?" before asking, "What is wrong?" That is the kind of support that kept me in the game. Also, I had a praying grandmother to whom I dedicate this book. This woman selflessly raised me to go after every dream my heart desired, all while never judging me on my mishaps. So, on June 26, 2020, not only will I present my bachelor's degree from Full Sail University to her, but I will also be giving her this legacy that she was instrumental in me creating.

I know you will enjoy this story of dedication and redemption, and I can't wait to hear and read all of your reviews. So, I am not going to hold you up any longer. You have a twenty-year journey ahead of you. Who am I to delay you any longer? To summarize my journey, I have to quote the legendary Tyler Perry and say, "People ask me all the time, how did you make it? I say it in the press all the time, but people cut it out…it was nothing but the grace of God."

Thank you for purchasing this book. Enjoy!

I Didn't Choose the Arts; The Arts Chose Me!

Growing up in North Philadelphia, I witnessed my share of crime, poverty, homelessness, broken families, and drugs. Just like many of you, I was raised by a single mother, but I lived with my grandmother. Some people would say I had the best of both worlds. I was blessed with a grandmother who honored and celebrated her grandson.

As I kid, I was very creative and enjoyed bringing people together for a great time. With all the sadness around us, why not create moments of laughter, enjoyment, and fun? With my creative mindset, I did just that. While we were out shopping, I would often ask my grandmother or mother to purchase party supplies from the local dollar store. The party supplies were not to celebrate anything; they were so I could decorate the basement. The basement was my man cave, my place of creativity. It was medium-sized and did not have a lot of stuff in it, but it was the perfect size to create my stage of fun.

Everything in the house became some form of decoration or a prop that would add just the right touch to my masterpiece. When I got older, my grandmother shared with me that I used to take my mother's pantyhose and use them as party streamers. I would drape them across the room and hang balloons from them. Talk about being creative! Once all the decorating was complete, I would get my mom or grandma to invite people to attend my party. Well, really to come see my work. Like great supporters, people would come, and we enjoyed food and fun under my decorations. To see the smiles on everyone's face was so exciting to me that the basement was my forever platform.

Another cool thing about my creativity is it allowed me the opportunity to direct and manage my mother and grandmother. In those moments, I could tell them what I needed, where I needed it, and how long it could stay up. Having that kind of power as a kid was huge. It gave me confidence in my ability to plan, and I had a great team that was willing to assist whenever asked. As an added benefit, I did not have to pay them. Now, who can beat that?

As I created and my designs improved, I became the official decorator for any party we had, including my birthday parties. The practice the basement provided gave me a keen eye for detail, colors, textures, and themes at a very early age. It was like I was previously an event planner and interior decorator in a former life. I took the gift and its enjoyment and ran with it. It wasn't until I started attending the Universoul Circus that I felt the need to up the stakes and transform the celebration into live entertainment.

Universoul Circus

Attending the Universoul Circus was one of my most memorable experiences as a child. Not only did I love clowns, but the entertainment and production quality were over the top for me. Being a kid with a vivid imagination, some of the things they would do, from dancing to the cultural music and then the crowd participation, excited me. The soul train slide and seeing smiles from both adults and children made me want to mimic that in the basement. Now, I knew I could not have elephants and tigers in the basement, but I could add dancing and change up the decorations to give it more of a stage-like feel.

Universoul Circus was the first live production I had ever witnessed, and I looked forward to going every year. As soon as I saw or heard the advertisement that they were coming to town, my requests to attend started. I never had any worries about someone forgetting, because Uncle Johnny, who is now deceased, was an usher for the show. He also worked with the ringmaster's sidekicks, Zanda "Zeke" Charles and Casual Cal. So, with his connections, I knew my seat was secured. It was always something about this production that, even in my older years, made me want to witness and be a part of it in some way. I don't know if it was because it was created and operated by African Americans or if because I was guaranteed to see people like me in the audience enjoying the show that drew me in at a young age. What I do know to be true is it introduced me to every element of the ARTS. Even today, I have such a love and appreciation for this circus because it opened my eyes to the possibilities of what could be. Plus, it showed me the power of creation. It introduced me to every aspect, from music, to dancing, to production, to set designs, to props, to a crew, and the audience. That right there was my oyster. That was life for me and having that was on my to-do list, but how I was going to make that happen and in which area was not quite defined. So, my quest to discover my lane started and my exploration of the arts began.

The ARTS Grew

By the time I started kindergarten, I had discovered a secondary love of entertainment, and that was the Philadelphia Thanksgiving Day parade. The Universoul Circus had the entertainment and production concept, but the parade gave me great costumes and floats. Man, the creations they made were amazing. You mean to tell me you can take cardboard, decorative paper, lumber, lights, and streamers and make a creation that I can ride? Who came up with all of this greatness?

As a kid, I sat there watching, absorbing it all and taking notes. Once again, I knew I could not bring floats in the basement. So, I would create processions in my grandmother's bedroom, pretending her bedpost was skyscrapers and the floor was JFK Boulevard. With my toy cars, trucks, and stick-figure men, I would create a procession and move them along the parade route. It got more interesting when I used washed clothes for flags. I know, I know. It's a bit much, but when you are allowed to be creative, you go the extra mile. Plus, surprisingly, my #1 cheerleader never yelled or discouraged me by making me clean up. She would come in the room, clap, and step out of the way so she would not stop traffic.

When my youngest sister, Keyona, was born, it was time to turn up. Once Keyona got a little older, I immediately added her to my imaginary payroll. She was my actress, student, and helper. Basically, anytime I needed assistance, she was summoned. Since we were having fun, she never said no. With her, I was able to practice my instructing and directing skills. I told you this was a family affair, but I was only discovering my lane.

By this time, I was attending St. Martin De Porres Catholic School on 23rd & Leigh, and the school's art program allowed me to see the behind the scenes of what I had been enjoying watching. For so long, I mimicked what I saw and recreated it in the basement. It was at St. Martin's that I learned the whys and hows of this industry. Like many of you, I had only witnessed the final result. St. Martin's, however, introduced me to the hard work and grit needed to sustain. The funny thing is, with all the excitement of the circus, the parade, and my basement renditions, I was not 100% sold on what I wanted to do. So, I started signing up for everything and anything that would have me. I did stuff I knew I did not want to do, but to say I'd experience it was way more important to me than to wonder what if.

First, I signed up for a performing arts class with Bro. Kenny and another one of his colleagues who would come to our school to teach production elements. Secondly, I signed up for acting and performed in the school production of *The Whiz*, where I played an ensemble cast member. Third, I signed up for the choir. Now, let's be clear. I had no desire to be a singer, but I used this traveling choir as a means to explore further. Moreover, a lot of the catholic schools we visited reminded me of the movie *Sister Act 2*, and I was always ready to jump in and sing "Joyful, Joyful". Of course, that never happened. Lastly, I joined Ms. Goveia's Dance School, where I learned tap, modern, and jazz. None of these areas did I truly master, nor did I spend more than a year in them. When I quenched my desire to experience an area, I exited stage left. Although still not sure what I was going to do with what I had learned, I knew it would have something to do with the arts, but what?

Death Changes Lives

I know you are saying to yourself, *This kid had too much free time on his hands.* You're right. School, home, and the basement were the extent of my journey, but I did have a best friend whose name was Isiah. We both had this thing for the arts. He was the first person, outside of my grandmother, that truly understood my passion. Even though it wasn't clearly defined, he knew I would end up doing something pertaining to the stage. Unexpectedly, Isiah's father decided his time here on earth had to end. Losing my best friend to murder left me closed and afraid to make friends out of fear that their parents would murder them, as well. This was my first experience with death, and it made me more sheltered. I knew my neighborhood was not the greatest, and my grandmother would remind us of that whenever we would ask to go outside or different places. After that happened, I didn't mind just doing my own thing in the basement. Sadly, I did not befriend another person for a long time. To this day, I am still cautious about who I let into my life.

From three to nine years old, the basement served as my self-haven; it was my first office and stage. Who would have known it would be the unofficial start of what would later become D. Richardson Productions? Are you inspired yet? Keep reading.

It's Time to Grow Up

September 11, 2001 – the day life changed and the shift from the basement happened. Around this time, my mother married her first husband, and we moved around the corner from my grandmother's house on Fifth Street. The basement, as I once knew it, became a distant memory. However, I was able to apply my decorating skills during Christmas time when my mother's best friend Sharon would come over. We would decorate our house and then go around the corner to hook my grandmother up. I enjoyed hanging the lights and watching how, after adding the ornaments and garland, it was a perfect masterpiece. As you can see, everything involving creativity excited me.

When we started visiting my mother's friend, Wendy, her daughter Brittany and I were plotting on her basement. From one basement to another, I know! They lived in Mt. Airy, and their house was way bigger. The extra space and deck gave us performance options, and it helped that she was just as interested in the arts as I was. We put on shows and hosted different events, and her friends couldn't wait to come over.

Things escalated with our productions at her house. Not just because she had space but because she also had the internet. Can you feel my excitement through the page? Of course, the internet was slow because it was dial-up. But, at my grandmother's, we did not even own a computer. Basic television programming was my friend, and at that time, I was okay with it. If we had grown up with the technology of today, do you know where we could be now? Me, either. So, I will continue with the story. Using Yahoo, we used to search for more ideas and concepts to create originality and performance-based theme during our shows. When I tell you, they weren't ready.

In addition to web surfing, we created playlists by using the website LimeWire to download and burn CD's to play. This was long before paid subscriptions such as Tidal and Spotify. To get the supplies we needed, we would also hold iced tea sales to raise money. Once we had our performance material and concepts, we held talent shows in her backyard. Oh, we were producing and executing before we understood what we were truly doing, and we started getting paid for it. As people joined us, our research grew, and Radio Shack became our friend. We created budgets and everything. We were strategizing every move from:

- The Initial Plan
- Materials Needed
- Creating a Budget
- Available Cash on Hand
- Who Was Responsible for What
- Show Day

We wrote and planned everything accordingly so there would not be any mishaps, and it helped that her mother and her mother's boyfriend at the time, Tony, were very supportive. Tony was a police officer, and something about his spirit drew me to him. He was more like a dad to me. He was genuine in his caring for me and always concerned about my well-being. This whole environment at Brittany's created great vibes, good learning, and tons of fun. Today, Brittany is a celebrity graphic designer who creates covers, posters, and other artistic works.

They Say You Can't Choose Your Family

Award-Winning Author Harper Lee once said, "You can choose your friends but you sho' can't choose your family, an' they're still kin to you no matter whether you acknowledge 'em or not, and it makes you look right silly when you don't." This saying couldn't be further from the truth. Although my mom and grandma both raised me, my experience with my grandmother was more enjoyable than my time with my mother. By early 2012, we moved to 18th & Cheltenham Avenue, and to delay my transition, I asked to remain in Catholic school. Thus, I stayed with my grandmother, only visiting my mother on the weekends until the end of the 4th grade. I was then transferred to Rowan Elementary School and moved in with my mom.

Just like at St. Martin's, I went back to exploring. This time, I was introduced to instruments and reading music. I played the clarinet and cello to tap into my music interest. When my mother saw the potential, I attended the Germantown

Settlement School to further hone my skills on the cello. However, I fell in love with drums and ballet. I added them to my new list of goals.

After one year, I was transferred to West Oak Lane Charter and completed 6th through 8th grade there. West Oak Lane added pieces to the puzzle that I was building about the arts by introducing me to my African American culture.

The Journey Starts

By now, I had tried my hand at dancing, singing, acting, and playing instruments, but I still wasn't sold on which one would prevail. I was still exploring to find my niche. I never let go completely of my creativity from the basement, but I needed a new outlet. That chance presented itself at Mira's birthday. Prior to this, my family was always looking for entertainment to have at her birthday party. One year, she had Jazzy the Clown with Tweety Bird. By the time her next birthday arrived, I had volunteered my services. Lo and behold, they agreed. Talk about being happy. HA!

As soon as I received the job, I asked my grandmother to take me to the dollar store to get some balloons. I used my silver Jordan sneaker case as my party box and loaded it with balloons, water, and party streamers. I had no idea what I was doing, but I knew we would have a great time. I recorded cassettes of Power99's "Drive at 5" mix so we could have music for dancing. I was set! I did not dress up as any character. I just performed and danced, and the kids had a ball. Why can't all gigs be this simple? But, anyway, I wasn't nervous or anything during the event. Every performance and celebrative moment was orchestrated and happened as I had planned. After successfully pulling off that party, I was ready to book more clients. So, my business mode kicked in.

By this time, I had my own bedroom, which I eventually transformed into my business office. There were papers everywhere. Still attending the Universoul Circus, I began studying their signature clown, Onion Head. I must say, the Universoul Circus is the backbone and the reason why I love arts, thus I make many references to them. From being introduced to Universoul Circus to now, the foundation of knowing what I wanted kept me grounded during the quest for my assignment. Plus, it gave me the standard on which to build my future. So, as I grew at West Oak Lane Charter, I kept that energy with me and excelled in all areas, from education to entertainment.

Shortly after attending West Oak Lane, I was invited to go to Bermuda with our student exchange program. It was my first international trip, and I was super excited. The trip was for seven days, and we learned about their culture and lifestyle. When we touched on the African culture, it sparked an interest. Thus far, this was the realest education about my people that I have learned. No, I am not from Bermuda, but hearing about African people in roles other than slavery and police brutality made me feel like I had a chance. I learned that we come from a lineage of queens and kings. We created a lot of inventions and were indeed people of high achievement. WOW! This was game-changing for a kid like myself who grew up in North Philadelphia and was a product of a broken home. Blacks were often written off as a statistic by society. So, to hear this gave me hope.

Excited about what I had just learned made me sign up for the black history show once we returned to school. I didn't care what role I landed. I was still on 100 from the power running through my veins. Once the parts were given, I was full of excitement. I was assigned the role of Nelson Mandela. With all the fire I had within from the knowledge I had gained in Bermuda, I knew I had to teach and embody Mandela, and I did just that. All I can remember was the audience clapping after my performance. Just like I did in the basement, I felt in my lane. That instant gratification from the audience made your boy feel like he had found his career choice, but then it was destroyed.

After all of the performances were done, the next thing heard was the sound of African drums. The music caught us all off guard, and then I saw what would be my next exploration. When that stilt walker came down the aisle dancing, I lost my mind. Between the music and this tall man, I was mesmerized. I remembered seeing stilt walkers at the Universoul Circus, and it was in this new moment that I wanted to become a stilt walker, too. At the time, I did not know what or who they were. I just knew I had to get on one. I later learned they were a part of the Imhotep Institute Charter High School African dance group. "Sign me up," I said. My mother officially thought I was crazy, and my grandmother told me, "Boy, you are not walking on no stilts." Little did they know, I was not asking for permission; I was putting them on notice. When it was time to apply for high school, what do you think was listed? You got it! I applied at Imhotep Institute Charter High School for no other reason than that stilt walker. When I got accepted, I did everything but that.

My Passion Was Challenged

For me, high school was both a gift and a curse. I was engrossed in the arts and fighting for my dreams all the time. From the jump, my passion was challenged, and I had to adopt the concept of "Nobody will stand up for you better than you." It was unfortunate that I was fighting my mother and her husband.

After we relocated from West Oak Lane to Mt. Airy, my stress level was on 150. In my eyes, my mother seemed like she had no interest in supporting my dreams. When I arrived home from school, instead of asking how my day was, she met me with, "When are you going to get a job?" Suddenly, it was like my passion for the arts was wrong, and she was willing to do and say whatever to make sure I let my dream go. She would even talk to her friends about me as if I was a problem child. In my heart, I knew I wasn't. I was just a child who appreciated and enjoyed being creative and performing.

Even now, I find myself waking up to hearing her mean words and remembering her hurtful actions. How could a mother fight against their kid's exploration of what they enjoy? If we had been homeless and I needed to step up to help pay bills, I would have understood her lack of support, but that was not our life.

My mom tended to put her men over her children. Instead of learning and standing up for her children, she would give the perception that we are the reason why her life or relationships were not flourishing. We became her scapegoat. Now, don't get me wrong. My mother was a provider and got us everything we needed. However, when it came to showing emotional support and love, she wasn't present. I can remember when I was at the height of my creativity and finally finding my lane at Imhotep Institute Charter High School. Instead of being happy for me, she always reminded me, "You need to go get a real job. Why don't you go work at McDonald's or something?" That was one of the hurtful things in my life that had a lingering effect. I honestly would have loved a bond with my mother, but I could not accept her outlook on life. I have nothing against employees, but I know I would not make a great candidate. Plus, doing something I love is what life should be about, right? I still can't honestly say I have a close relationship with my mother, and I am at peace with it. Even now, I often wonder if her breaking down was really over a job, or did she not want me exploring what she could not understand?

Being the first one in my family to embark on a career in the arts, I knew it would not be accepted by many. Therefore, I needed to grow tough skin against the naysayers and doubters. Was I supposed to get this much heat from the one person, if no one else, who should have believed in me? Just a thought! Granted, I understand my mom's rationale was to raise me with the tools she knew would guarantee me a means of survival. Even though I want to forgive her on that merit alone, my heart is constantly reminded of just how hard she tried to break me down. To make matters worse, my defiance when it came to my working led to her kicking me out of the house.

I can remember an incident when I was arguing with my mother's husband. He grabbed me and ripped my shirt. I don't know if I was mad that he gripped me up or because he ripped my new shirt. At the time, I was working with one of my uncle's girlfriends, Kim Marshall, who had a food program, and with the money I earned from her, I would buy my clothes and sneakers. When that man ripped my shirt, I tore his shirt, too, and out the door I went. For the next two weeks, I stayed with my godmother, but then I had to go back home. One would think we would sit down as a family and get things straight. Nope! It was back to business, as usual. Instead of fighting them for love and support, I buried my energy into the arts. Imhotep became that beckon of safety for me while protecting my vision.

Imhotep Saved Me

Lacking support at home, I started searching outward in hopes that I could find either a role model or a parental figure who understood me. While at Imhotep, I found the biggest support in one of my teachers, Baba Tyrone Davis, and the founder, Mama Christine Wiggins. Being our leaders, they were there to serve in all capacities. Gaining their wisdom was key to building up the confidence my mother was tearing down. Since I could not accept defeat, I leaned on those who appreciated the arts and understood what a difference in having a career in the arts could mean to me.

The more I learned from them, the more active I became in the various activities. I joined the amazing African dance company that sold me over at West Oak Lane Charter. I also joined the drum team and once again tried my talents in the choir. At this point, with all the fighting I was doing at home, I knew I had to become successful in the arts. So, it was time for me to revisit my days of doing shows in Brittany's backyard and remind myself of the smiles on the kids' faces at Mira's birthday party. I also giggled while thinking about the first play I penned with Brittany called *Ghetto Cinderella*. When I tell you, we tried everything before the age of fifteen. This had to work. The best part is, in addition to teaching and putting a lot of emphasis on the arts, they also taught us the importance of ownership and entrepreneurship. At that moment, my conscious was clear, and I was finally ready to take this journey seriously. I was still not sure what area of the arts I was interested in, but I knew I had great respect for performing and entertainment. So, focusing on those areas became my priority, and learning the concepts of entrepreneurship became the prize.

Then I got hit with a curveball. When I was getting in alignment with my goals and strategizing on a plan, I got introduced to Tyler Perry. Drop the mic! The game plan now had to be changed. He used to showcase his plays at the Merriam Theater in Philadelphia. I was always so angry that I was not allowed to go. As a treat, my mother would purchase the DVD's, and I watched, studied, and learned how to create and keep a great storyline. In my head, the man is my uncle. I am waiting for the day that I finally get to meet and thank him for opening my eyes to what a professional theatrical production looks like. I remember watching *Madea's Family Reunion* and *Diary of a Mad Black Woman* and thinking to myself that he makes it look so easy. However, remembering my performing arts classes at St. Martin and watching the behind-the-scenes work at the shows in which I had performed, I knew that perception was far from the truth. But it's what I wanted to do!

How was I going to incorporate live theatre into my performing and entertainment strategy? I mean, I could audition for one of his plays. I could write to his fan company every day until he replied to me. Or I could stay focused in my lane, learn the craft, get some dirt under my nails, convince him to create a job for me within his company, and then we could take over film, television, and theater. Now that would be huge, right? I have this mantra: *I am going to create a job for myself in your company.* Not to sound cocky, but I know my commitment and love for the arts. I knew what I could offer, and it has always been my goal for people to see the value in my exploring and utilize my expertise. By this time, I had learned the job positions of everyone in the arts, from the janitor to production stagehand. This kind of knowledge is priceless. Hearing this man's story of how he can run every job in addition to performing, singing, writing, and making people laugh, I was inspired. Yup, that is what I was looking to do.

To dive into this element and learn more about the theater world, I went back to learning scriptwriting and attended the New Freedom Theater. Imhotep had a partnership with the New Freedom Theater, where they combined their performance arts classes to perform collectively during their winter showcases. While there, I had the pleasure of working with Patricia Scott-Hobbs, Antoinette Gilmore, Diane Leslie, and a few others who ran a program that taught the fundamentals of theatre. One of the shows that I truly enjoyed performing in was *Blacks on Broadway*. I had a dance routine that I performed in the *Step into the Bad Side* scene, and from that moment, I grew to have a strong respect for musicals. This production allowed me to see how you can incorporate dancing, singing, performing, and entertainment into one script. The overall production was high energy and something I had never seen. Tyler was great, but this musical lane was sparking another interest. I remained in my lane and merely continued absorbing it all.

By connecting with the New Freedom Theater, I was able to do my internship there to complete my senior thesis. I was capitalizing on all relationships and showing up in ways that made me stand out.

During my time at Imhotep, I received not only an education but also the chance to create a vision of my future. They provided me the opportunity to learn, explore, and travel. From the New Freedom Theater to opening for Dr. Maya Angelou and visiting Ghana, I soon came to realize they were more than just an excellent school for stilt walkers. Did you see me slide Dr. Angelou and Ghana in there?

So, let's go back a few. During my ninth-grade year, our dance group was given the honor of performing at the National School Conference held in North Carolina, where Dr. Angelou was speaking. To perform and then hear her speak was truly life-changing. Dr. Angelou is a legend and a staple in the arts. As a graduation gift my senior year, I was afforded the opportunity to visit Ghana, West Africa, for two weeks. This invitation came because I secured a 3.7 grade point average, graduating number two in my class. In addition to the trip, I was awarded a full scholarship, so there was no cost to my mother. While there, we did a lot of touring. We visited slave castles, learned about their culture, and attended many events and gatherings to see African dancing.

From stilt-walking to witnessing Africa, Imhotep owes me nothing. That school created a path and gave me the tools and resources to start this journey well equipped. From understanding the arts to appreciating the value it brings to the African American community, they confirmed my commitment to what I had dreamed of in the basement. I still had a decision to make regarding how I was going to incorporate my love for performing and entertainment with theater. Instead of harping on the how, though, I focused on what would be next for me.

I still remember when The University of the Arts accepted me into their multimedia program. I knew deep down this was not aligned with my ultimate goal, but, hey, it would give me the opportunity to learn the skillsets connected to a digital camera operator, film and video editor, dubbing editor, sound effects editor, audio recording engineer, and more. Even though I could have used some of this in either performance or entertaining, it was merely another exploration. Plus, I received a partial scholarship, and some free money made this extremely appealing.

After one semester, I changed my major to theater technology and started preparing my life to produce my very first theatrical play entitled, "Girl He Love Me". While Tyler Perry was creating, I was ready to take that leap of faith. As I was jumping to produce, I stopped attending classes, and my schoolwork suffered. So, I had to make a decision. When I decided to return to school, my professor made it for me when he said, "You might as well drop out. You will never be nothing in this industry."

After hearing him tell me that I could have done one of two things: punched him the hell out and filed a complaint (because he was a white man) or drop out and prove him wrong. What do you think I did?

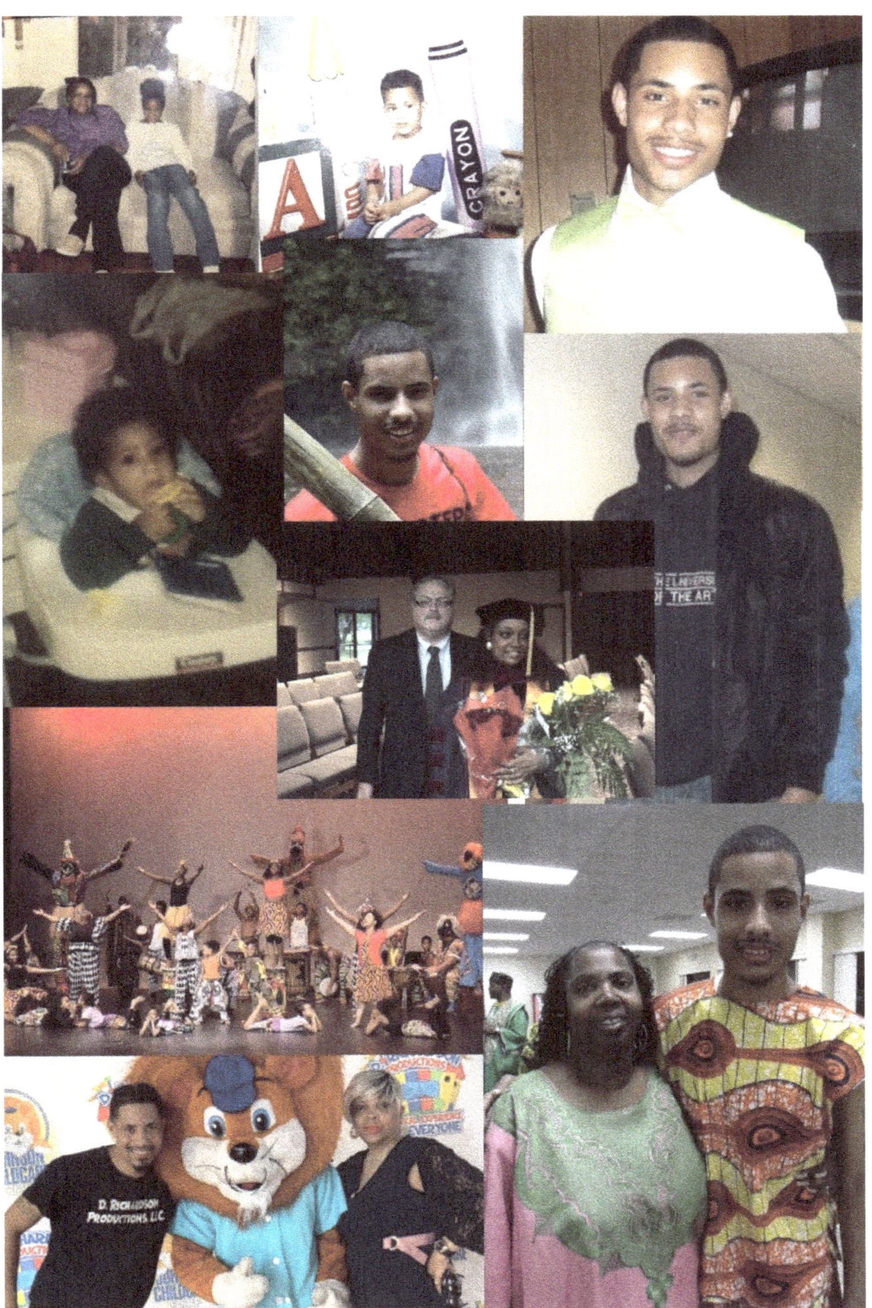

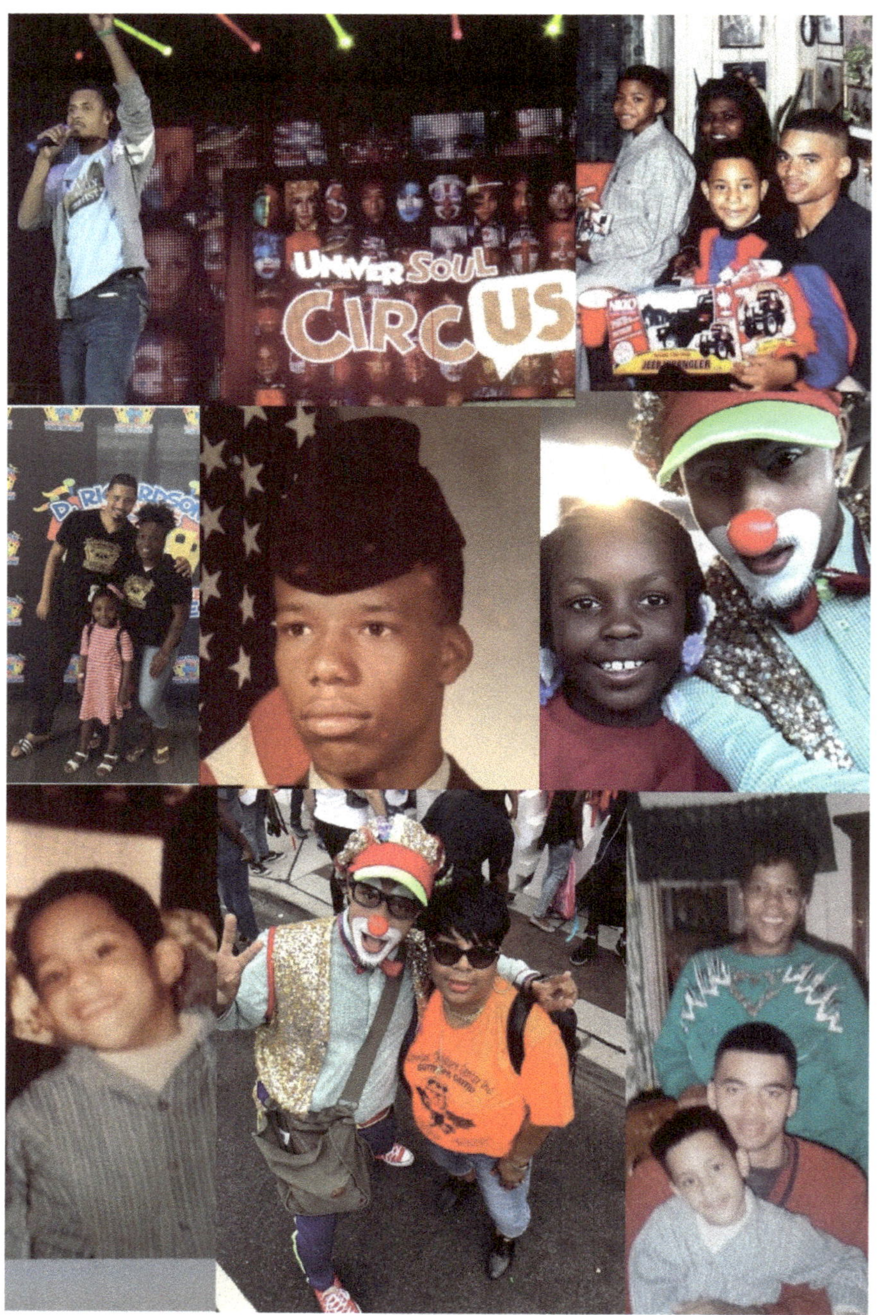

UNIVER SOUL
CIRC US

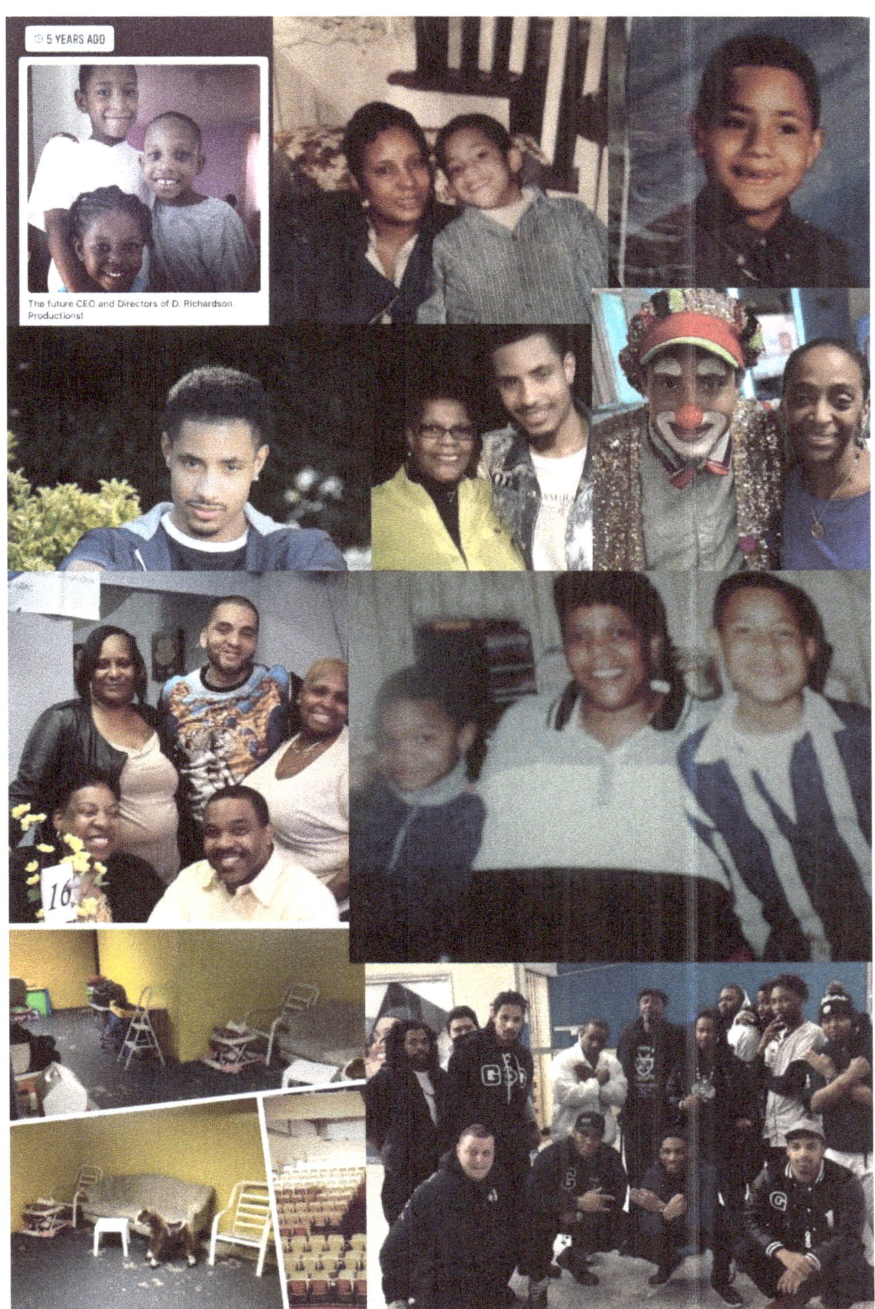

The future CEO and Directors of D. Richardson Productions!

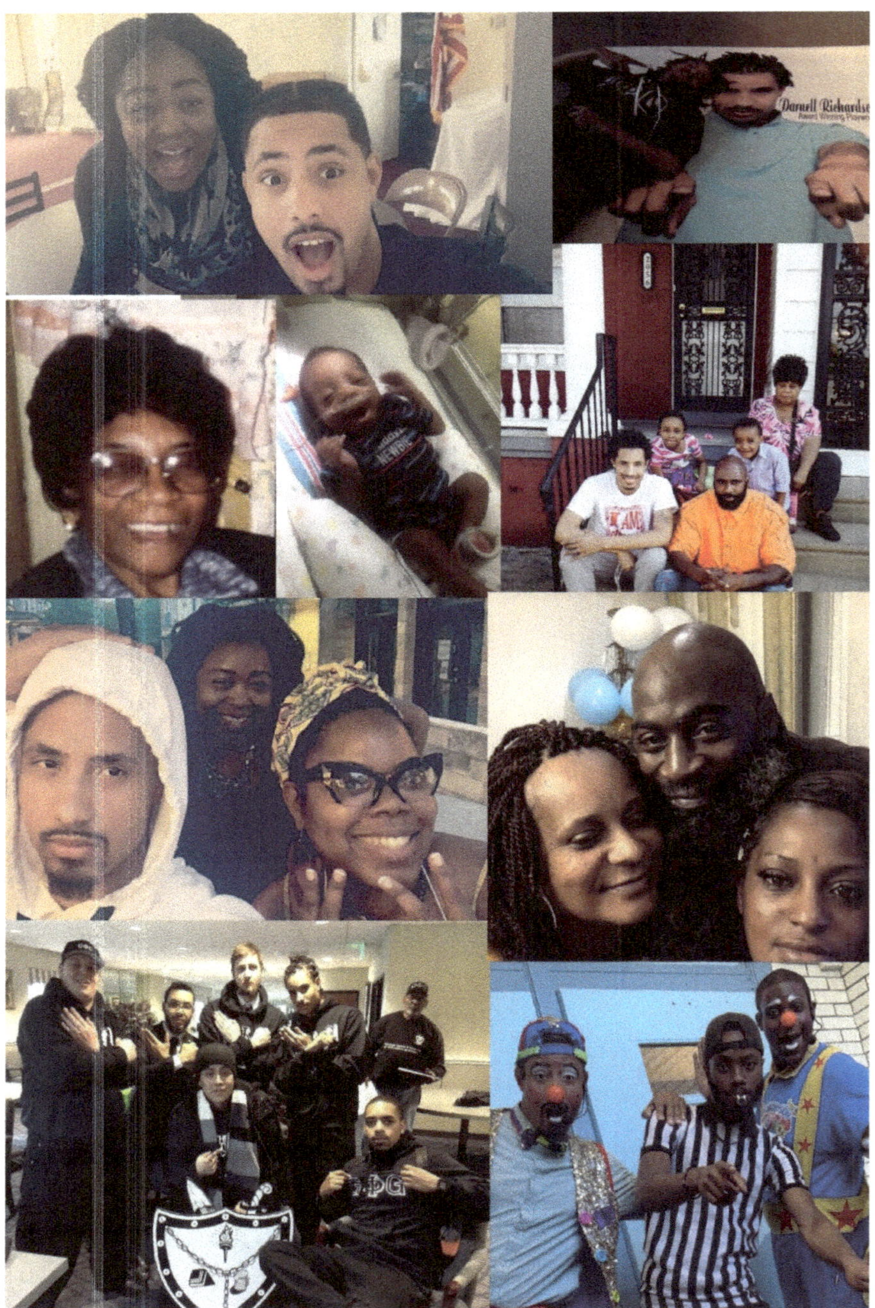

Darnell Richardson
Award Winning Playwright

My Road to Entrepreneurism

You might as well drop out. You will never be nothing in this industry. Just writing that statement makes my blood boil. Who did he think he was to tell me who I am or not in this industry? You're probably thinking, *Well, you were missing class.* Well, I could have missed the whole semester, but that did not give him the right to count me out of the game before I stepped foot into the ring. Plus, hearing him utter those words immediately made me relive what my mother and her husband used to tell me:

Go get a regular job!
You don't know what you are doing!
Why don't you play football or a sport?
Go work at McDonald's!
You are not good enough!

Why was my one dream such a threat to others? First, it was my mother, and now this professor was discounting my ability. That was it! I was tired of defending my dream and my right to explore. Since he represented The University of the Arts, I knew that institution could not serve me any longer. So, I dropped out! The good thing was I had a play that needed my attention. Maybe his ignorance was a blessing. Why question God, right?

By leaving The University of the Arts, I was able to start building on my foundation of performing and trying my faith in theater. Even though I could have done this while in college, I was not looking forward to being in another classroom or having to deal with a toxic professor who thought it was cool to tear down his students. I focused my drive on starting my own company by way of introducing people to Darnell Richardson, Jr. I had some people to prove wrong, and then there was myself who deserved everything that was coming to me. The year 2010 marked the beginning of a new era for me. Even though I did not receive formal education nor knew how the business worked, I was ready to dominate the stages of Philadelphia and beyond. Before we move on to the entertainment, let's explore how I embraced entrepreneurship and why this element of working for myself was so necessary for me.

And In The Beginning

My peek into entrepreneurship started with Ms. Kim Marshall, my uncle's ex-girlfriend. She owned and operated a daycare center and a food program. My mother served as the director of her summer camp, and I hung around to watch and learn. Ms. Kim was my crash course into the world of self-employment. Seeing how she managed both businesses and enjoyed life on her terms made me interested in learning more.

While I was hanging around and asking questions, Ms. Kim immediately started putting me to work, explaining what I was doing along the way. From filing applications to speaking with clients, I was intrigued at how she handled her business and thought to myself, *This is why she is so successful.* She knew what to say, and her clients loved her.

As business picked up during Ms. Kim's peak season, I went from applications to learning how to build a portfolio, structure a business, write contracts, and prepare documents. This learning experience gave me the tools of entrepreneurship and the foundation I would need when I started my own business. It was while working with her that I saw just how much money a person could make working for themselves. Also, I learned how having a reliable team helps with managing your life. That right there was living to me. As a teenager, I could not comprehend working for someone to help make them rich and then looking forward to getting reimbursed for their work that you did. I mean, how do you work for thirty, sometimes forty-plus years to save up for retirement that is supposed to guarantee you the same life for the last ten to fifteen years of your life? That did not make sense to me. Ms. Kim gave me the opportunity to serve her, and I took it as God's way of introducing me to my future.

After working with Ms. Kim, I created multiple businesses geared toward various areas in the arts that would either fund my dream or put money in my pocket. While in high school, a friend and I created a clothing line called Yung Star Fashions. We would use bleach to create different patterns, along with tie-dyed shirts. With the time being during the stonewash era, it was trendy. Our clothing was seen in several of the fashion shows at Imhotep, which was always a great thing. Shortly after that, I created an organization called Philadelphia African Americans Scholars Hold Action. This organization provided the youth with a platform to be the voice for their peers. We were often offered speaking engagements and attended events that focused on the youth and our need to be better citizens of the community. Even though I was young, creating this platform gave me the ability to hone my speaking, marketing, and pitching skills. This organization lasted for about a year. By then, I was ready to get back into performing.

Since I was in the dance company in school, I figured it would be a great idea to start my own company to gain extra exposure and eventually money. With my big aspirations, I needed to find ways to fund them quickly. Since I had a group of like-minded peers, I was able to pitch the dance group idea and get people to join. Initially, this group was not formed for its income-producing potential. We just wanted to entertain. As we got better and people started enjoying us, we would get bookings and receive donations. We performed at shows, block parties, and any event we were called to do. As long as it was legal or had no adult content, we were there. This exposure eventually led to people asking us how their kids could be a part. As folks inquired, my brain started moving, and what was supposed to be a hobby became the start of our dancing school. Who would have known that by adding four new kids, we would have to teach? This is where my time with Ms. Kim paid off. Because of her training, I could arrange bookings, choreograph, and show up to do what I loved to do.

As we grew, I knew it was time to make the group official. Thus, creating what was to become my first business, African Connection Dance Company. One of the member's father has an organization called The Help Organization with which we partnered to do shows. The one good thing about this group was that everyone associated was also connected with someone who could elevate our goals, mine especially.

In addition to performing and booking, I started revisiting my scriptwriting days with Brittany. I also held performing art training and formed another dance group called Movement Elite. I accomplished all of this while in high school, but this particular group grew and evolved into my adulthood. Since we were well into the computer age, I was able to create websites and market our business online. I was always creative when it came to flyers and marketing material, so creating ours was a breeze. I understood very early that for you to grow in business, people need to know you exist. I was creating a brand.

Practically overnight, things went from quiet to being booked. We secured our biggest opportunity to perform at the Academy of Natural Science during the grand opening of a new exhibit. It was free and only for a weekend, but to me, none of that mattered. Every platform was a steppingstone, and at this time, all events were great resume boosters. To create the perfect show, I started employing people to help with the production, choreography, and performing. The crazy thing about my hiring process was that everyone I hired was older than me. I was ready to explore a universal brand, and I knew that by hiring older, more experienced individuals, we could get the job done. Plus, it was time to level up. If I could perform at a well-known museum, then it was time for the world to know who Darnell Richardson Jr. was. Thus, causing me to create a more universe performance company. I immediately changed the name from African Connections Dance Company to the unofficial name of D. Richardson Productions. This was the beginning of my career, my future, and my hard work.

D. Richardson Productions

Let's take a minute to reflect! Wow! Can you believe just how much I have accomplished? All of what you've read occurred when I was between the ages of three and eighteen. Even though you are probably thinking I did more exploring than accomplishing, I can most likely agree with you. In fifteen years, I had tried everything. I created opportunities and stopped. I joined groups and quit. The one thing joining, exploring, and trying did for me was it helped me narrow down my lane. I knew I loved the arts, but what style? What part? Was I going to be a performer, dancer, writer, or entrepreneur? I had learned early on never to limit myself. There is no written gospel that says you can only be good at one thing, and there is no law that states you can only try one area of any industry. I am truly blessed to have attended schools during a time when the arts were still prevalent. These outlets gave me the ability to release my creativity and channel it into something greater than me. I don't know about you, but something about the arts makes me feel free and alive.

Now that I had the unofficial foundation for what would soon be D. Richardson, I was ready to try my hand at theater. Even though, I was mimicking Tyler Perry and using what I had learned in St. Martin's, West Oak Lane, and at The New Freedom Theater, I was ready to explore this theater network. Now remember, I had no formal training with writing scripts, theater production, or the business dealings of a theater. I did, however, have enough confidence in myself to pull this off. As I noted previously, my very first play, *Girl He Loves Me*, premiered in 2011 at the Walking Fish Theatre in Philadelphia. I hadn't quite stabilized the business concepts and dealings of D. Richardson Productions. So not wanting to falsely showcase an incomplete company, the play was listed as "a play produced by Darnell Richardson". I used this production to ensure it was something I wanted to do before I invested money into it.

This play was very heavy, as we addressed the ills of domestic violence. In the story, Tracy Scott found herself in a relationship with a guy who she thought loved her. With people around who encouraged her to move on in life, Tracy refused to face her reality of being a victim of domestic violence, and it almost cost her everything, including her life. We did three shows in one day and sold out soon after advertising. The Walking Fish Theatre was a small, intimate theater in the Northern Liberties section of Philadelphia, holding thirty seats. I know you are like, "Thirty seats! Come on, Darnell." But, to me, this was a huge accomplishment, especially with it being my first professional show on my own. Plus, in that one day, ninety people were introduced to my work. Not bad for a kid who had used toys and stick figures as his audience years ago.

When it was time to fund the play, I used my money and the earnings from the show. From my time at The New Freedom Theater and by speaking to others, I learned that you can generate funding by selling tickets, pushing ads, and selling vending space. Back then, the theater rental was only about three hundred dollars. So, between my vendor fees and ticket revenue, I was able to pay the production off easily. My actors and stagehands were volunteers, so it worked out well.

The success of this play made my head big, and I knew there was no turning back. However, even in my excitement, I had to take a step back and re-evaluate how I was handling the business. Looking back, I can honestly confess that even though this play was a success, quite a few hiccups occurred that could have cost me. For example, a door fell and crushed the finger of my volunteer make-up artist. She ended up suing the theater, and the theater sued me, as well. Remember, I was eighteen years old at the time. I was not educated on liability insurance or protecting my brand from lawsuits, so this was very scary. If it had not been for my grandparents in Christ, Dr. Linda & Gary Gusoff Esquire, I don't know what I would have done. I swear, God knew who to send during my time of need. Pop Gary was a lawyer, and he represented me. After having a conversation with the other attorneys, it made sense that I, personally, didn't have anything to do with it. It was not due to my negligence that she got hurt. Thus, this lawsuit went away. Being faced with that experience taught me that having creativity is not enough to produce a live production.

There was a lot about the business that I did not know. If I wanted to save my reputation, it was time I take this more seriously.

Securing the Bag

Immediately after being saved from that lawsuit, I applied for my LLC, a limited liability corporation. At that moment, I realized I could not allow my dream to bankrupt me. So, I stepped back for a minute to truly learn the business of running a business. I wanted to be legit. God must've known I was a good steward because he blessed me with the opportunity to bring *Girl He Loves Me* back for an encore. This time, we went from a 30-seat theater to a 100-seat theater. We kept our 3-show run, and I can remember thanking God.

When I visited the Adrienne Theater, I would get so excited thinking about how close I was to the Merriam Theater, where Tyler Perry brought his plays. The progression was exciting, but then I ran into my set of hiccups with the Adrienne. During one of the shows, the circuit in one of the lighting boards went out in the theater. As the director and producer, I had to think quick. How can you put on a show with no theatrical lighting? People were waiting for the house to open to take their seats, and I could not delay them. So, instead of canceling the show, we did the whole show with the house lights – no red, blue, or green. It was no different than you sitting in the living room watching a show. Tacky, I know. But, hey, people enjoyed the show, and no sweat was dripped.

Even though things in this business started rocky, quitting was never an option. Now don't get wrong, there were times back then – and still to this day – where I was like, "This is a lot." I have caught myself considering finding a 9-to-5 a few times, but then I come back to reality. I think of it this way: no pain, no gain. If it were easy, everybody would be doing it. Therefore, I take my ability and creativity, and I keep pursuing my goals. Plus, if I got a job, I would be decreasing my income and time. Being an entrepreneur, I have the ability to make as much or as little money as I want. Quitting now would make every sacrifice worthless. At this time, I can't afford to gamble with that kind of risk. Therefore, I have created a strategy that has kept me soaring in business and learning the ins and outs of the industry. That strategy was monetizing the power of networking.

Do you know that people are your greatest stock when it comes to pursuing your dream? They connect you with the right people. They promote your services and products when they approve of them. They will invest in you when they believe in your work. People are your lifeline when it comes to building, marketing, and maintaining a business. Throughout the years, people have been my biggest help when it came time to get things done. From networking to partnerships, the biggest reason I was able to do this was because of the people who would not allow me to quit. This concept was also huge when it came time to selling and booking shows. Those scheduled for my shows invited a whole new network; thus, creating new investors for me. For example, if I hired an established actress in the industry to perform in one of my plays, some people would only purchase tickets to see her, not because they knew me. Moreover, she would be bringing her network, friends, and family.

You must be strategic when collaborating with others. You can both benefit and win big. As I mastered this, I noticed an increase in ticket and merchandise sales, the vending slots being filled, and requests from people to bring my productions to their cities. None of this would have been possible without the relationships I built along the way. It was always a joy to work with people who understood that connections were more important than a paycheck. When people yell, "I don't work for free," I often respond with the question, "Do you want to work for the moment or a lifetime?"

This is Not What I Signed Up For

Around this time, things were coming together. I knew what I needed to do as far as my goals. I was connecting with some great people and getting the support that I needed, but my personal life was spinning out of control. I was accepted into colleges but then dropping out or getting expelled. I was trying to make ends meet to survive. I understand all too well when people say, "When it rains, it pours." I needed to see some sunlight if I was going to stabilize my emotions in this season. If there was ever a time when I truly wanted to throw in the towel, it was then.

I had completed a great run of my play, *Girl He Loves Me*. I was also picking up different entertainment work and still moving the dancing school, but I was swamped with building the business without any real knowledge and direction on what was required. This, by far, took up a lot of time and interfered with my ability to work and be secure. I did not want to work illegitimately or be ill-prepared. So, as always, my education was not my top priority, even though education was what I desperately needed. Since I was self-employed and nobody was volunteering to pay my bills, the business had to remain in the forefront. I was adamant about not being an employee, so I had to make this work. To justify my college failures, I would say, "My mom didn't go to college, so I don't have to either." I know that was wrong, but, hey, I had to tell myself something.

Suddenly, the pouring turned into a major thunderstorm, and the energetic life I was building humbly crashed. At about twenty years old, I was in a major car accident. Even though the accident led to a payday and my first apartment, I was eventually forced to leave my place and move to Delaware with my grandmother in Christ.

Now, I am not going to say I mismanaged the money, but paid business was not coming in as fast as the bills or the money I spent to keep up. When the keeping up started costing me my sanity, it was time to step back and regroup. I even picked up a job as an independent contractor at a local charter school as a performance arts instructor. The money was good and filled in some of the gaps. However, the more my finances struggled, the more I knew I was doing something wrong. So, when I moved to Delaware, it was indeed a wake-up call.

My grandmother in Christ, Dr. Reverend Linda Gusoff, was the spiritual support I needed during this time. She gave me space and time to figure all of this out. Plus, I was able to help her around the house with chores, running errands, and things of that nature. Who moves out of their mother's house only to move back in with someone else in about a year? That person would be me. I know. I can feel the judgement, but trust me, I have already said everything to myself that you are probably thinking. I praise God that I had people who were concerned with my well-being more than they were with why and how I got myself into that situation. To add to my circle, I pledged Groove Phi Groove at Delaware State University and fit right into a brotherhood that supported me as a person. I am not going to say I was trying to find myself, but I used this period to self-reflect and get my life intact.

As things started looking upward and business was rebuilding itself, I faced another challenge Commuting from Smyrna, Delaware, to Philadelphia and back was becoming taxing. I was also presented with the opportunity to work with The Steve Wilko Show by running promotional trips to the live studio tapings. This served as another stream of income that I used to prepare for my big return.

Even though I had to humble myself and ask for help, this moment gave me a perspective on time. Delaware allowed me the ability to witness life from a different pair of eyes. Growing up in North Philadelphia created the foundation of learning how to entertain within the realms of poverty. Living in West Oak Lane and Mt. Airy showed me that you could struggle but be highly connected. Regrouping in Smyrna offered me the peace to find myself. Although I was not making as much money as I had in the past, I finally had the peace to plot and plan my best move yet. Being removed from the inner city made a world of difference, along with that hour-and-a-half drive daily. It gave me time to think. It was like God sat me down to breathe life, wisdom, and confidence back into me. He knew that if I had continued to explore without a plan, I would eventually crash and burn. So, I took my last ounce of dignity and birthed what would make me unstoppable.

The Rebirth

Support saved me. From business trips to recitals at the school, Darnell Richardson was making his comeback merely on the support of others. Even though no one knew all that I was facing, they came when I needed them. I am forever grateful to my friends, colleagues, and other peers who showed up for me on desperate calls for prayer, investing, or volunteering their services. During this time, I was faced with the harsh reality that not all my family was as supportive as I expected them to be. Now, Aunt Kathy, Aunt Nicole, and my grandmas never missed an opportunity to support, but four people out of both my maternal and paternal relatives were hardly enough when it came to my vision.

It always seemed very strange to me that those who shared my DNA could celebrate and believe in other people's children more than they did with me. To find comfort, I convinced myself that their failure to support was a result of my being the first child in my family to travel down this path of performing and entrepreneurship. I took it as their lack of understanding or wanting to see proof before they approved. Most of my family members worked in the mental health industry, the federal government, or as nurses and teachers. They were all career and professional people with a 401K and benefits. Here I come rebelling against the lifestyle they knew worked. Even though we did not agree on career paths, it would have been nice for them to step outside their way of thinking and believe in me. I did not always know what to do, but with their support and maybe a few ideas, it could have made some of my dark nights brighter.

Sadly, I accepted my family's lack of support. I knew that if I was going to excel, I needed to go where I was wanted and nurtured. As I began seeing life through a new set of lenses, I wanted to be around people who appreciated me for trying. If for nothing else, they saw my effort and wanted to see me happy. I was tired of the fan pretenders! You know, the people who pretend to support and celebrate you, but in all honesty, they are jealous and waiting for your downfall. They only come around to see how far you've come or how close to destruction you are. I had to change my whole circle while protecting my new space and energy! Plus, when I understood that my business success is a direct reflection of my personal growth and mindset, I had to get selfish and use the power of "No, thank you" as I moved forward.

As I was rebranding, I found my niche with social media and how to use the platform to grow D. Richardson Productions effectively. I quickly elevated my power of marketing and partnered with new networks, creating new platforms to build clientele and offer support to the community. In 2019, I created a non-profit entitled I AM the Arts Foundation. The goal was to raise funds to cover the expenses of those children who wanted to join one of the programs but could not due to financial restraints. With the arts being removed from the schools, and remembering how vital it was in my creating and building character, I want every child to be afforded the same opportunity.

In addition to this, I joined the Michelle Snow network, which placed me around other great entrepreneurs and offered me the ability to share my gifts. I was able to generate clients to assist with marketing. I was hired to create tote bags, flyers, and other various marketing material that would put their businesses in the limelight. From that network, I joined another group, The Vendors Club. It was there that I became the marketing guru. Those clients not only used my services, but they also became clients by vending at my events, selling the bags and shirts that my company had created for them. The hustler in me was born. I refused to lose! I went to my network, created networks showing them how I was vital to their brand, and then gained new clients. What did I say earlier? *I am going to create a job for myself in your company!* People don't know what they need until you show them what they don't have. It was this moment when D. Richardson was formally created as the company to every entity with which I was working.

The Start of a Legacy

As I was reorganizing, I realized there were many moving parts to this thing I called a business. I had the dance companies, Movement Elites and Dance 4ever, and the theater component. It was time to create a parent company, if you will, to represent all parts as one company. When you go from performing in museums to opening for Beyoncé Knowles in front of the Art Museum during the Made in America concert, what other direction can you go but up?

Plus, I had new networks and clients all over with my marketing services. It was time to build what I always knew was possible.

Even though D. Richardson Productions became active in 2010, I was operating all entities separately. So, I started merging and redefining what every platform represented, creating what Disney is now to ABC. Every brand I had ever built was given a new home and purpose. I created three tiers for the dancing program, educational piece, and the entertainment packages with affordable packages. In addition, I hired a team of dancers, administrative personnel, and directors to run each segment. Doing so allowed me the opportunity to expand the company to gain more clients and exposure.

Through everything I have done, my goal has always been to provide professional and affordable training to all individuals. We now have two locations in Philadelphia, and I am currently working on Florida and Georgia expansions. I am even looking at some international locations. I refuse to let politicians write off the arts and have also included other programs to our roster, such as photography, self-defense, modeling, and acting. We even offer rental space for community events, birthday parties, and more. With D. Richardson Productions, it is my goal to provide what my generation did not experience or simply give the kids an outlet other than violence.

If you go to any urban community in America, you will see there are few outlets for fun. They've removed the libraries. Recreation centers are becoming a thing of the past, and sports are only offered in areas where you can find people who are willing to coach. We have erased the childhood experience that once kept us occupied after school and during the summer. If I can keep at least one kid off the street by teaching them a new dance step or catwalk pose and then watch them pursue it afterward, all of this exploring and hard work will have been worth it. Under the new D. Richardson Productions, our tagline is "The magical experience for everyone." We want everyone to feel like a kid again by achieving something they always wanted to explore.

The Big Return to Adulthood

It was time to come home! My foot was on the gas, and I knew I needed to create another entity that would be my primary stabilizer. My bread and butter, if you will, came when I started my family entertainment services. This service offered clown and magic shows, cartoon characters, face paintings, balloon bouncers, and the hosting of birthday and carnival-themed parties. I was able to create any theme while making a kid's birthday or any other event magical. We also included our rental space if the customer did not want to host at their physical residence.

This entity grew relatively fast. We had major community support and partnerships. Two of our significant partnerships were with Saudia Shuler from Country Cookin' Restaurant and Johnson Childcare Center. These two connections led to bigger opportunities, and the owner of Johnson Childcare Center, Elaine Johnson, became my guardian angel. She allowed me to use her space to host my events and plays while I was generating money and new clientele for her.

My sister, Patricia Curry, was also very helpful. We worked together at the West Philadelphia Achievement Charter Elementary School. She was my right hand. Whenever I called on her to do face painting, make funnel cake, or teach our dance program, she was there. Stacy Philips, the CEO of West Philadelphia Achievement Charter Elementary School, was also heaven-sent. She offered her school space to us at no charge. She also gave me marketing ideas and taught me how to promote within the community, from supermarkets to gasoline stations. Because of her assistance, we were everywhere.

Work was stabilizing, and money was becoming more consistent. It was time for me to return home. Until I was 100% back on my feet, I stayed from pillow to post. I lived in Delaware for about two years, but working late nights in Philadelphia and then commuting while sleepy wasn't adding to my bottom line. I had a friend in the entertainment business who, at times, let me stay with her. This kind of instability made me feel homeless and caused me to grind harder to get back to my own. I know you are once again thinking, "Why not get a job?" My best answer to that is I tried but wasn't hired. During this rebuilding phase, I completed applications to get some stability, but they never worked out. I applied to Target and Walmart, but for some reason, they would not hire me. I took that as a sign for me to tough it out. I got me into this mess, so I had to get me out of it.

Ms. Elaine showed me her business strategy, and it changed the way I operated business. Before her, I would just book clients and deliver with no plan or purpose; I just went to work. She gave me a method that made it easy to maintain my life and operate a business.

One day, Ms. Elaine taught me not only how to handle money, but how to never be without it again. She made me write down my cost of surviving and then how much money I needed to live happily. Whatever those totals were, that is how much I needed to make monthly. That method truly helped me because I was able to see what I needed for living and what I could keep for myself. After building up my living income, I was ready to go back out and reintroduce myself to adulthood. Soon, I was manifesting every dime I needed to make payroll, pay expenses, and pay myself. I knew exactly how many kids I needed in class and how many bookings I needed to gain profits to make all of this work. So, with a game plan in place, the stress of money was erased. I was better able to give myself a new start.

This humbling period lasted about four years, but I am proud to say I have my own address, a flourishing business, money in the bank, and I travel to Miami for leisure every other month. I am finally doing me!

What Did It All Teach Me?

With everything going on around me, what did I learn? Did I understand the importance of mastering my gifts? Did my exploring delay me from the bigger success that I missed by starting and stopping a given opportunity? Often, I sit back and analyze everything. I reviewed the organizations and relationships I started one month and ended the next. Where did I go wrong? Did my exploring cost me what God already had prepared for me? Then I realized that even though my exploring had a funny way of teaching me life, the lessons attached were the greatest gifts. Throughout this journey, I learned the importance of staying committed, remaining humble, appreciating opportunities, and facing troubles with grace. These four concepts saved me from a lot of breakdowns.

To be honest, the one thing I regret is leaving The University of the Arts. I was someone who received good grades in school; a dropout is not who I was. How did I allow that man's opinion of my future to make me defer what I was supposed to achieve back then? Did I put my dream over my education? As bad as it sounds, I did. If given the opportunity again, I wouldn't change anything.

You see, being a kid who had been told for years that I would not make it in this business, I felt it was time for me to prove myself and my worth. I could not build a business and secure a degree at the same time; it wasn't possible for me. My dream was more important than a piece of paper. For years, I kept my business as my #1 priority. School couldn't meet my needs.

After leaving The University of the Arts, I attended University of Phoenix to major in Business. After six weeks, I quit because the classes were more lecture-based and less interactive. I was not interested in being talked to all day. Then in 2012, I started my journey at Full Sail University. This was the third school, and they say the third time is a charm. So, I was going to make it by default, right? Wrong! I started off great. My grades were excellent, and the teachers loved me. I was enjoying my progress, but then the business started slipping, money was lacking, and my survival was in jeopardy. My grades suffered as a result of me focusing solely on the business. My grade point average dropped, and eventually, Full Sail withdrew me as a student.

Wait! Did they just kick me out? Oh no! What am I going to do? It was one thing for me to leave on my own accord, but being dismissed was a feeling I had never experienced. One that did not sit well with me at all. Even though my business demanded much of my attention, I could not accept Full Sail's decision. So, after a year, I appealed. They eventually let me back in, and things once again were great. But then, the business needed me, and my grades dropped. Soon after that, I was kicked out again. The second time did not upset me as much as the first because I thought of it this way: I was doing what most people were going to school to do. I was already living and achieving what we were studying. I was managing a business, drawing up contracts, networking, and pitching. I was the heart and money generator for D. Richardson Productions. If I was not working and creating, I was not eating, and my team would leave.

In 2018, it became evident that I needed my degree. The levels to which I wanted to take my business required a different kind of education. So, instead of seeking out another school, I humbly went back to Full Sail, pleading for one last chance. I started the appeals process and was completely honest about why my grades were low and how I was in a better situation to finish this time around. I wrote letters and sent in documents to prove that I wasn't wasting time but needed this degree to propel me personally and professionally. It took a year for them to approve my request, and I am finally getting my degree on June 26, 2020.

From 2012 to 2018, I deferred my education to survive my way. I could have easily gotten a job to make ends meet and remained in school, but where would that job have eventually led me? I am the kind of person who will not be deterred from my goal by defeat. Yes, I kept putting myself in situations that cost me another opportunity to excel, but I was a kid who was accustomed to exploring and leaving. I knew the only time school would work for me was when I desperately needed it. Even though it would have been helpful in 2012, it is required for my elevation in 2020.

I've Won Because I've Stayed in My Lane

If you take nothing else from this book, please comprehend this important fact: "What God has for you, it is for you." As an entrepreneur and a business owner, I have seen too many people create a product, business, or script, and right before they market it, they delay the process because they believe the marketplace is too congested. Now, before we move on, let's understand the idea of congestion. Since the beginning of time, there has always been multiple people who possess the same abilities, gifts, and talents. You had people who could sing, others who could write scripts, and tons of business owners. They never worried about what the next man was doing or viewed them as competition. They broke bread and called them a friend. In my opinion, only those who compete with others or who are not 100%

confident in their ability look at a congested market as being troublesome.

Throughout my journey as a writer, performer, and entrepreneur, I have encountered people who tell me that I do too much. "Why do you do so much?" they always asked, and I would reply to myself, "I haven't even started yet." As an entrepreneur, creating lanes and building new opportunities is your kryptonite, and trying to get paid for it is the reward. In today's society, who can survive doing only one thing? It has been proven over and over again that our economy is unstable, and the government is unreliable when it comes to the way they handle poverty and employment. So, now I operate with multiple "active" streams of income. "Active" is the key word here because I need every stream to generate income so I can secure a profit after paying all expenses. Remember, my many businesses are my paychecks. I clock into myself, thus leaving me responsible for my survival. When it comes to a congested stage or crowded marketplace, I create my own lane and generate my own customers, leaving me competing against no one but myself.

Tyler Perry once said, "God gives everyone a lane, and no one can beat you in your lane. Just stay focused on Him and what you are supposed to do. And everything will be alright." This quote is the mindset I used to obtain this level of commitment when it comes to building my business. I am comfortable in knowing that D. Richardson Productions is not the only entertainment company within the tri-state area. I appreciate the fact that I am not the only performer in Philadelphia. I am delighted when I see playbills that feature other actors. When you know what you are and who you are in the industry, you can enter a crowded room and still gain attention from the guests. This requires a great mindset and a secure business that is tangible and profitable. Do you have that? Allow me to offer you a look into my mindset and business checklist that will help you own your place in any room.

- Walk in like you deserve to be there.
- Learn the industry and know the key players.
- Defend your territory.
- Reaffirm your mission.
- Ensure your business solves a problem.
- Ask yourself how your business serves the community.
- Seize the moment.

Even though you are the face and brand model of your business, you also need to make sure your business operations are tight. When you are standing in a room full of executives and leaders, the last thing you want to do is show up ill-prepared or not prepared at all. Do you have a team that you can trust? Do you have a business plan with a five-year forecasting model attached? Do you have available funds that you can use to secure that theater for your next show? Your business must be as on point as your readiness to take over the congestion.

As far as the arts, you can explore many opportunities to generate income by working in areas you are good at doing. For example, if you can sew, you may want to pursue being a costume designer or starting a clothing line. If you have taken acting classes and performed, you could be an acting coach or offer advice to people pursuing the industry. You can even create your own lane and make money doing what you love.

During my travels where I connected with people, I have learned that many people in the arts are not clear on some of the most important areas that need to be mastered to "make it" in this business. Some people question me on whether to go to college for entertainment or learn through experience. Others want to know how their business strategy should look. So, I want to use this time to give my opinion on these issues. We will call it free coaching. If you ask one hundred people the same question, you will get one hundred different answers. So, don't take what I am saying as gospel. I am, however, a person who has experienced it and is currently profiting from it.

Formal Education vs. On-the-Job Training

When it comes to formal education versus on-the-job training, I am all for college education, hence me graduating with a bachelor's degree soon. To be honest, you can have a degree but gain more knowledge doing the job. No textbook can teach me how to prevent a play from failing when a cast member doesn't show up the night of the performance. I have never read in a book how to handle being homeless while pursuing your dreams. There are just some things a book cannot teach you. There is a saying, "Experience is the best teacher." I must agree. Everything I know is based on 75% on-the-job training and 25% education. However, formal education does enhance your ability to charge higher rates and capitalize on your gifts. Either is great, but when you have them as a collective unit, you are officially winning.

Networking

Networking is essential because you never know who you could potentially meet that will take your business to the next level. Networking is almost like building a team that is there to serve you by placing you in the right situations. However, networking can be very tricky because you can find people who say they are for you, but really, they are against you. Don't be naïve, thinking everyone proud of you will support you. My mother proved that one not to be true, but little did she know that her discouragement helped me to have tough skin that prepared me for the times when I would be disrespected or used later in life. You would be surprised how many people only networked with me to either learn my brand to mimic it or to stab me in the back eventually.

When it comes to networking and bringing people into your business, be careful, and truly understand their motives. Remember, your business is your baby, and nobody is more excited about its success than you. If your business were to fail today, it would fall on you solely. Your team would also blame you. Even though networking is a great thing, and I have used it to advance my career, it can also make you want to throw in the towel and walk away if you connect with the wrong people.

Marketing

When it comes to marketing, we have used billboards and postcards. However, social media is, by far, the best form of marketing today. It gives you a broader reach with the share option and boosting ads. Your business, products, and brands have a much better chance of being seen by thousands of people, and it gives you the ability to communicate almost immediately with a potential client. Plus, people are visual and buy based on validation. Social media gives you the best of both worlds.

Since this has been a big winner for me, we will be offering social media services soon. Our services will range from managing accounts to creating content. Trying to survive in this industry has taught me the importance of marketing. People can't support your business if they don't know it exists.

Pricing

In the beginning stages, I did not have set prices simply because it was more of a passion than a job. I would often tell people to give me what they could afford. However, as I started accruing expenses, I had to think about pricing and what would be considered too much or too little. Eventually, I felt if a person liked it and enjoyed it, I should charge the value. It took some time for me to get to this level, though.

One thing about the arts, and most other industries, you must serve before you seek success. I am not saying you have to work for free, but there is a saying that is truly important here: "You have to pay your dues." I believe Kevin Hart says it this way, "Everyone wants to be famous, but nobody wants to do the work." The entertainment business requires you to do the grunt work before you drive the Benz. It's just proper protocol. If you are just starting in this industry, my suggestion would be to focus on learning and being an assistant before jumping for the executive job. You are always a student in the arts because it's an ever-changing industry. Pricing is important because that is how we take care of our families. However, if pursued too early, it can be the downfall of your business.

Building a Team

Making sure everyone was on the same page with my vision and goals was key when building a team. People work with and flock to people who can help them achieve their personal goals, but at the end of the day, people who believe in you and know that if you win, they win should be the only people assisting you. Far too often, we build teams with people who are only in it to advance their careers. When team building, look for those who possess integrity, motivation, knowledge, and passion. Find your common interests and their ultimate life goal. Building a team requires conversation and communication. It is more than just cutting paychecks and sending 1099s.

End Scene! The Next Chapter

Wow! Impressive, right? I have read some memoirs where it took them a lifetime to achieve and lose what I did within a twenty-five-year timeframe. Talk about getting stuff out of the way. Even though my journey was full of trials, success, overcoming, and rebirthing, I am a man committed to my goal despite having a mother who tried to deter me and a professor who attempted to break me. The theatre almost got me sued, and I remained diligent in my pursuit of what I had created in the basement. God did not offer me the opportunities to serve, work, and perform for me to walk away from it all. I believe there is a bigger calling on my life.

So, what's next for me? Well, how much more time do we have? Just kidding. Great news! I will be graduating from Full Sail University on June 26, 2020, with a bachelor's degree in Entertainment Business. I plan to use this degree to create a public relations entity within my company, where I service corporate clients. With all the experience I have on a local level with marketing, producing, and creating, I feel that with a degree, I will be well-equipped to help executives excel and generate millions. I am no longer interested in the bottom line. It's the year 2020. We need to create our own lanes and work with people who can help us achieve above and beyond our profit margin. This may sound a bit far-fetched, but in case you haven't noticed, everything I do is unconventional.

Even with all that I have accomplished, there is so much more I still want to achieve. I would love to partner with Tyler Perry. I can't wait for the day when I get to have my own family and create memories with them. I am grateful for the many opportunities I have been given. There are many nights that I sit and think, *What if I had listened to my mother? What if I would have given up on my dreams? Would I be further in my career if I would have obtained my degree at The University of the Arts?* I have a lot of questions, but I am grateful that even in my broken and hungry days, I did not allow the pressure of making it kill me.

I want you to take everything I have shared with you and think about your stagnant gift or talent. What career did you bury? Les Brown once said, "The graveyard is the richest place on Earth." It took me years to understand that saying, but as I got older, I learned the graveyard is where you "find all the hopes and dreams that were never fulfilled, the books that were never written, the songs that were never sung, the inventions that were never shared, and the cures that were never discovered. All because someone was too afraid to take that first step or not determined to carry out their dream." Truly understanding this message made me decide between my gift and the naysayers because I knew a nine-to-five was not in the cards for me.

So, remember this. Even if you are working a job, you can still manifest your dreams. I know tons of people who are still working a nine-to-five but are living out their dream by utilizing their gifts or passions. With the pressures of the day-to-day hustle of life, wouldn't it feel good to be able to do something you enjoy and possibly get paid for it? Wouldn't you feel more inspired or worthy of life if you were living to enjoy it instead of only living to work and eventually die?

The graveyard is the richest place on Earth, but it doesn't have to be. Use my testimony to motivate you, and if you need my coaching services to help you enjoy your gifts on this side of Earth, then I can help you with that. Trust me, doing so will be far more rewarding, fulfilling, and legendary for you and your family than you sitting on your dreams. For me, the greatest reward received after tapping into my gift is the fact that my future children now have a business that they can collect on, work for, and operate for the rest of their lives. Even after I depart from this earth, they will continue to receive royalties from everything I established. My businesses are now inheritances that will carry them and the generations to come. Although my mind was taught to work for a pension, my journey to D. Richardson Production has allowed me to create something that will outlive me and sustain others even when I am in the graveyard.

Thank you for reading!

About the Author

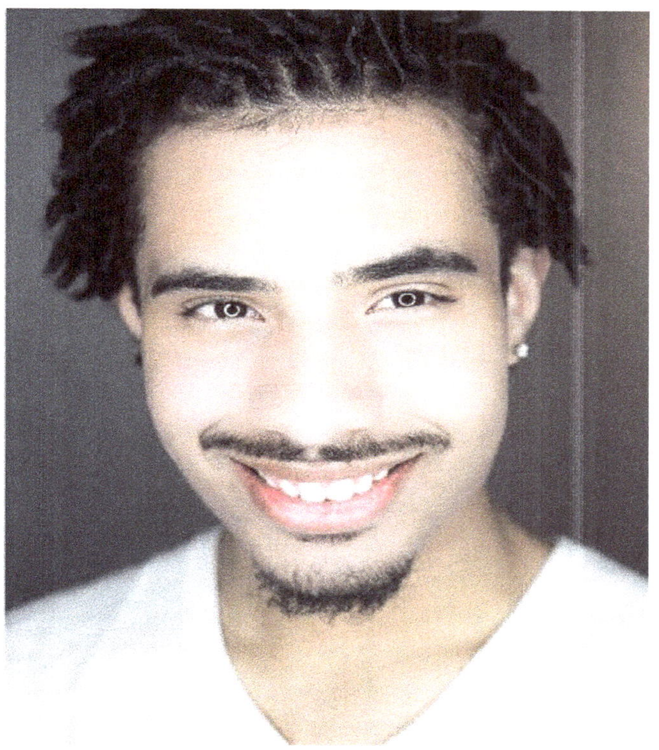

Darnell Richardson, Jr. grew up in North Philadelphia. From the time when he was a little boy, Darnell has been cultivating his love and passion for the arts. This multi-talented artist comes with an arsenal of talent. Darnell is an award-winning playwright, producer, and has produced three theatrical productions entitled *Faith of a Mustard Seed*, *Girl He Loves Me*, and *The Reassurance*. *Faith of a Mustard Seed* was later recognized in the Peach Theatre Awards and won Best Musical Production. Darnell's work has been seen around the world in such places as Atlanta, New York and Bermuda.

Darnell's talent doesn't stop there. He is also a choreographer and proud owner of D. Richardson Productions Dance Academy formally Danse4Ever Studios, established in 2012. Darnell has used this platform to create and develop programs that will provide professional dance education to his community. Darnell's D. Richardson Productions Dance Academy brand has been featured on Fox29 Good Day Philadelphia, 6ABC Thanksgiving Day Parade, Odunde African Festival, the Universoul Circus, South Jersey Caribbean Festival, Philadelphia 76ers games, and I Am a Philly Artist TV. Darnell is also a proud member of Groove Phi Groove Social Fellowship Incorporated.

Mr. Richardson looks forward to the future and his endless possibilities. No dreams are too big for the young rising star!

Darnell currently makes home between Smyrna Delaware, and Fort Lauderdale, FL.